RADIOLOGY JOURNAL

THIS JOURNAL BELONGS TO:

THE RAD LOOK

Made in the USA
Columbia, SC
04 March 2025

54705075R00061